Beautiful Birds

ROBINS

By Kristen Rajczak Nelson

Gareth Stevens
PUBLISHING

Please visit our website, www.garethstevens.com. For a free color catalog of all our high-quality books, call toll free 1-800-542-2595 or fax 1-877-542-2596.

Library of Congress Cataloging-in-Publication Data
Names: Rajczak Nelson, Kristen, author.
Title: Robins / Kristen Rajczak Nelson.
Description: New York : Gareth Stevens Publishing, [2023] | Series: Beautiful birds | Includes index.
Identifiers: LCCN 2021035982 (print) | LCCN 2021035983 (ebook) | ISBN 9781538275283 (set) | ISBN 9781538275290 (library binding) | ISBN 9781538275276 (paperback) | ISBN 9781538275306 (ebook)
Subjects: LCSH: Robins–Juvenile literature.
Classification: LCC QL696.P288 R35 2023 (print) | LCC QL696.P288 (ebook) | DDC 598.8/42–dc23
LC record available at https://lccn.loc.gov/2021035982
LC ebook record available at https://lccn.loc.gov/2021035983

First Edition

Published in 2023 by
Gareth Stevens Publishing
29 East 21st Street
New York, NY 10010

Editor: Kristen Nelson
Designer: Andrea Davison-Bartolotta

Photo credits: Cover Mike Truchon/Shutterstock.com; p. 1 David McMillan/Shutterstock.com; p. 5 Tom Biegalski/Shutterstock.com; pp. 7, 24 (beak) C. Hamilton; p. 9 FotoRequest/Shutterstock.com; p. 11 rwkc/Shutterstock.com; p. 13 Bonnie Taylor Barry/Shutterstock.com; p. 15 Nicholas Hylton/Shutterstock.com; pp. 17, 24 (nest) John A. Anderson/Shutterstock.com; pp. 19, 24 (egg) Alexey Stiop/Shutterstock.com; p. 21 Gabrielle Hovey/Shutterstock.com; p. 23 JPBC/Shutterstock.com.

Printed in the United States of America

CPSIA compliance information: Batch #CSGS23: For further information contact Gareth Stevens, New York, New York at 1-800-542-2595.

Contents

Robins are birds.
They are brown
and orange.

They have a yellow beak.

They are found all over North America. Another kind lives in Europe.

They live near trees.

They eat worms.
They eat berries
and fruit.

Many go to warm places in winter. They find more food there.

They build nests.
Nests are made of
grass and mud.

Mothers lay eggs.
Eggs are light blue.

Babies come out
of eggs.
They have few feathers.

They can fly about a month later.

Words to Know

beak

egg

nest

Index